Pearson
PUBLISHING

Student Handbook for
Art and Design

Richard Hickman

Richard Hickman has been a senior figure in art education for a number
of years. He has been responsible for the training of art and design teachers since
1985 and has experience as an inspector and senior examiner for art in schools.

Illustrations by Patrick Bullock

Acknowledgement

Other practising artists and art educators, who are experts in their own field, have
been consulted and have freely given their advice and expertise. These include:
Andy Ash, Michelle Bassett, Hemanti Chauhan, Louise Clark, Ben Crane, Lisa Henshall,
Richard Keys, Ruth Marriage, Charlotte Peel, David Reed and Jo Styles

Name ....

School...

Class ....

Exam board ....

Syllabus number.....................................

Candidate number ....

Centre number.......................................

Coursework deadlines............................

....

....

Examination dates ....

....

Further copies of this publication may be obtained from:

Pearson Publishing
Chesterton Mill, French's Road, Cambridge CB4 3NP
Tel 01223 350555   Fax 01223 356484

Email info@pearson.co.uk
Web site www.pearsonpublishing.co.uk

ISBN: 1 85749 637 X

Published by Pearson Publishing 2000
© Pearson Publishing 2000
Second edition 2002
First reprint 2003

Contents

Introduction

This *Student Handbook for Art and Design* provides you with support, advice and up-to-date information about art and design at Key Stages 3 and 4, and GCSE. The National Curriculum for Art and Design emphasises three connected areas – understanding art, knowing about art, and making or creating art. This handbook is based on these three areas.

The first part of the book deals with **understanding art**. This will help you to start thinking about art in a clear and informed way. It looks at what art is, gives some definitions, and considers aesthetics, rules, and art criticism and appreciation. It also introduces an approach you can use in order to understand artworks more fully.

The second part of the book, on **knowing about art,** gives an overview of some of the main art movements and styles. It looks at aspects of art history and issues surrounding the making of art. This will help you to show how your own work is connected to other artists' work. It also provides an approach for making your own Site-Specific Art.

The third part of the book, on **creating art,** is intended to supplement the work you do in school under the guidance of your teacher and to encourage you to experiment and be creative. It gives general advice on some materials and techniques, and on colour and using ICT.

What you understand and know about art should also help you with your own art-making – they are not completely separate! You should try to make use of your knowledge and understanding of art (past and present) to help you explore ideas and create different images.

This is not a 'how to do it' book – there are plenty of those for the many activities available to you in this subject area. It is more of a pocket reference book which will help you to put your own art-making into context; there are, however, a few examples of art practice to get you going. The most important aim of this book is to develop your ideas and your understanding – if you think like an artist, you are well on the way to being one!

The book also provides guidance on meeting National Curriculum/GCSE requirements, and a useful glossary.

What is art?

The term *art* can be confusing because it means different things to different people. *Art*, according to the National Curriculum, means *art, craft and design*. In general, we will use the same definition in this book, although we will often simply use the word *art*. But what is the difference between art, craft and design?

Art – expressing an idea or feeling

Art

Art usually means anything made by people which expresses an idea or feeling in a skilful way. It is sometimes concerned with beauty and is usually (but not always!) interesting to look at.

Craft

The word *craft* comes from an Old English word meaning strength. Someone who had a strength in a certain occupation was therefore

Craft – making something with skill

3

someone who had craft. Nowadays, craft refers to making something with skill and specialised knowledge, and often with imagination and creativity as well.

Design

Design comes from an old Latin word meaning to mark out. When we sketch out an idea for a building or a car, for example, we are marking out, or designing. Design can be defined as: 'the planning of visual elements, in order to solve a particular visual or spatial problem'.

Design – solving a particular problem

In addition to these general meanings of art, craft and design, we can use each of the words in more specialised ways, such as the design of a painting (referring to its composition) or the craft in a print (meaning the practical skill evident in the print, as something separate from its other qualities).

Aesthetics

Aesthetics is concerned with making judgements about art. It also involves asking questions about what is art and what isn't art – and what could be art.

For example, someone might look at an abstract painting and say 'that's rubbish – it isn't even art!'. This would be looking at the artwork *categorically*, because the person does not think it should be called art. Another person might look at the same painting and say 'this is a work of art', meaning it is very good compared to other artworks; this would be using the word *art* in an *evaluative* sense, since it is valuing the piece more highly than other work.

What is art?
What is not art?

Aesthetics, then, examines the nature and value of art. The main questions in aesthetics are:

- What is art?
- What is not art?
- If something is judged to be art, how do we judge its quality and worth?

5

Traditionally, there are three main ideas about what art should be, with related ideas about how it should be judged:

- Art should be based on **imitation**. It should look like something or represent something; the more realistic it is, the better the art.
- Art should be concerned with **feeling and expression**; the more it conveys feeling, the better it is.
- Art should be concerned with the **interesting arrangement of visual elements**. The most successful art is that which has the most 'significant form', ie the most interesting arrangement of shape, colour, etc.

However, a lot of art does not fall comfortably into just one of these areas; in fact, most art has connections to more than one theory. In addition, the three areas really only refer to what we might loosely call 'Western' art, that is art done since the Renaissance (c1400-1600), typically in Western Europe and North America (see pages 18 to 41 for more information on this).

Nevertheless, most of us have a particular idea about what art should be like. You might think it should be beautiful or realistic, or you might think that the most important thing is for art to be expressive – conveying the artist's feelings. Some people even think that anything can be called art if someone says it is, or if enough people say it is.

Art doesn't necessarily have to be liked by everyone, or considered by everyone to be 'good' art.

What you think about art is important, but make sure that you do think! In order to discuss or judge art, you will have to try to clarify your beliefs and ideas in order to find out whether they are based on sound foundations.

Breaking rules

Western art is sometimes concerned with commenting upon social issues, such as war and injustice, rather than creating art 'for art's sake'. It is also often concerned with commenting upon the nature of art itself. Sometimes an artwork is considered to be worthwhile simply because it shows a new way of looking at something, or uses materials or images in a novel way.

Of particular importance amongst contemporary artists is the idea of breaking rules, especially rules concerning what art should or should not be. This idea is expressed in the quote on the following page by the artist Ben Crane.

Break rules – get someone else to do it for you...

7

'it is very important to appreciate the weight of rule breaking... use water or glass or even words as works of art. Use humour... use new media and collaborate with other departments, blur the boundaries between science, art, music and English... side step the problem of painting by using random methods to create your art, get someone else to do it for you...'

Nevertheless, some activities which we might call art are done using strict rules by groups of people, with the resulting artefacts lasting only a short while. In some cultures, the value of artefacts is determined by the extent to which they conform to the rules, rather than the extent to which they are original. This is especially true in traditional art and design of the Indian subcontinent, particularly artefacts which deal with religious themes.

Here are some questions to consider when thinking about and judging art:

- Should an artwork be done by only one person?
- Does art-making necessarily involve having a practical skill?
- Are there special rules for making art?
- Should an artwork be made to last?
- Does an artwork need to be unique and original?

If we look at the artists featured in many books about art, we could also be forgiven for asking:

- Is art only made by men?
- Is art only made in the West?

Art has been produced by both men and women in all countries over the centuries but most of the artists you will have heard of are probably Western men such as Vincent van Gogh, Leonardo da Vinci or Andy Warhol. It is important to remember that this is largely due to historical or social factors, rather than male Western art being 'better' than other kinds of art. You should try to find out about female artists and art in different cultures.

Is art only made by men?

Looking at art

This section provides you with ways of becoming familiar with art, through art criticism or appreciation.

How do you first relate to an artwork?

Art criticism is concerned with ways of looking at artworks. *Criticism* in this context does not normally mean saying something bad about an artwork (although it can mean that!), but rather responding to an artwork in an intelligent way. See pages 15 to 17 for some question prompts you can use when looking at an artwork. There are different approaches to looking at artworks; the following '4R' approach is a useful one: react, research, respond and reflect.

React

This is your first reaction to the artwork: How do you feel about it? What does it remind you of? How do you 'relate' to it? You might well see a piece of art in a modern gallery and say 'my dog could do better than that!', which is a perfectly reasonable initial response, but you need to go further and ask yourself why the art object is in a gallery in the first place; are other people seeing something that you're missing? Note down your first feelings and ideas about the piece.

Research

This is an important second step, involving an examination of the artwork in two stages: firstly of the artwork itself; and then the circumstances surrounding its production.

The first stage of the research involves looking carefully at the artwork, either as a reproduction or (preferably) in real life. Examine the visual and tactile elements (colour, pattern, texture, composition, shape, form, line, space, tone) and their relationship to each other in the artwork.

(Refer to the glossary on page 93 to see definitions of these elements.)

You should look at the artwork's content – what is it about? Look carefully at what it is made of – what kind of material seems to be used? Is it a collage or a montage? Is it a painting or a sculpture? How is it put together? Is it made of metal? If so, what kind and why? Make a list of all the things you can see, dividing the list into different categories, such as 'subject matter', 'colour' and 'composition'.

Look at the artwork's content – describe what you see

The second stage of the research involves inquiry *without* the artwork. This is where really involved research can come in, and you can discover a great deal of interesting information. You could investigate the artist's intention, perhaps looking up things the artist has written about the artwork. You should look at the relationship between the content and the process, and the context in which the artwork was produced. If you are feeling brave, you might also want to consider the social, theoretical and philosophical issues which may have influenced it.

Respond

This third step is concerned with making a considered response, based on what you have discovered through your research (ie having found out about the artist and their circumstances, how do you now feel about the artwork? Has your opinion changed?). This is an opportunity for you to talk or write, in an informed way, about the artwork. Try to use an appropriate art-specialist vocabulary – some suitable words are provided in the glossary on page 93.

Reflect

You should now think again and contemplate the meaning and nature of the artwork in the light of all of the above. What does it mean to you? How does it relate to issues which concern you? It is important to let things sink in, to give yourself time to build upon what you have learned, and to think in depth about the artwork you have looked into.

Art objects, after all, are often made to have a significant, deep and moving effect upon those who look at them. Art has been, and still is, considered

to be very important for all cultures, since the
beginning of time – have you ever thought why?

Art is made to have a significant effect upon those who look at it

The approach described above forms a framework
within which you can learn more about art in a
structured way. It is important to become familiar
with the key concepts and specialist vocabulary of
art. If you have a rich and varied vocabulary
covering the visual elements in art, then you will be
more able to discover those things in art objects.

Notes to help you look at artworks

Your first feelings

Write down your first feelings about the artwork.

What do you think it's about?

Visual and tactile elements – Make notes on:

Colour

Shape

Form

Line

Texture

Space

Composition

Basic facts

You can usually find out the following fairly easily:

• What is its title? ....

....

• Who made it (artist's name)? ....

....

• When was it made? ....

• What is it made of (the medium used)? ....

....

Context and intention

Where was it made? ....

What else was going on at the time the artwork was made?

• Other artists

| |
| |

• Other art movements

| |
| |

• Technological innovations (eg oil paint, photography)

| |
| |

• Religious and cultural influences

| |
| |

Why was it made? ....

Who was it made for (who commissioned/paid for the artwork)?

....

Consider also the present context:

* Why was this work chosen to be exhibited? ....

   ....

* Who chose it? ....

   ....

* Why is it shown in this way? ....

   ....

Your response

What is your response in the light of your research?

Is the artwork successful?

Further notes

Consider also the time-span of the artwork – here are some
words for you to think about: longevity, duration, time-based,
real-time, ephemeral, temporary, permanence, change.
Note down any spin-off ideas for your own work:

Art movements and styles

Whether you know it or not, your own artwork is influenced by what has gone before.

The history of art is a huge subject area, and most people only know a tiny amount, usually about 'isms' like Impressionism and Cubism. However, both these art movements stem from Western Europe and occurred within the last 150 years; obviously there is a lot more art from other areas of the world and from different times.

Did you also know that Modern Art has been around for a long time and is not so modern? Most art historians would say that Modern Art began in the 19th century, with groups of artists such as the Impressionists experimenting with new techniques. Contemporary art, on the other hand, is work that is produced by artists living in our own times. It can be very traditional in nature, or it can be extremely unusual, challenging or thought-provoking.

Some contemporary artists include:

- Damien Hirst, who cut a dead cow in half and exhibited it as a sculpture
- Christo, who put wrapping paper around large buildings
- Tracey Emin, who displayed her unmade bed as an artwork
- Carl Andre, who became well-known for his arrangement of ordinary house bricks.

You can familiarise yourself with artists' work, and the different ages and cultures they have worked in, by:

- visiting your local art gallery or museum
- visiting Web sites devoted to art and artists
- reading art books
- cutting out and collecting articles about art and artists from magazines and newspapers.

By doing these things, you will also automatically develop your general and art-specific vocabulary. This is important! In an examination, you should be able to show that you can write about art, using an appropriate art vocabulary.

The following list of art styles and movements is intended to highlight some of the major developments in Western art. It is by no means a complete overview, but gives a brief introduction to some of the influential groups of people who have had an effect upon current attitudes. The list is shown in alphabetical order. Some of the movements are illustrated to help to demonstrate the style; these illustrations, as you will see, all have the same subject. In addition, reproductions of some actual artworks are shown on pages 33 to 36.

One of the problems of lists such as this is that they give the impression that all movements are of equal significance. It remains to be seen whether Installation Art will prove to be as significant as Dadaism, for example. In addition, a relatively small art movement such as Vorticism cannot really be compared with a large-scale tendency such as Romanticism (it could be said that most art movements in the past 150 years could be classed as Romanticism). Therefore, the major art movements appear in capital letters in the following list.

Abstract Expressionism

This is a style of non-representational painting which combines Expressionism with abstraction. An early Abstract Expressionist painter is Wassily Kandinsky (1866-1944); later ones include Mark Rothko (1903-1970) and Willem de Kooning (1904-1997). Their

paintings are typically large and bold, often with unrestrained use of colour. See also the 'action painting' of Jackson Pollock (1912-1956).

'Abstract Expressionism'

Art Deco

Art Deco is a style of design which became popular in the 1920s. It grew out of Art Nouveau, and is characterised by its geometric forms, rather than curving and flowing lines. Many cinemas were built in the Art Deco style.

Art Nouveau

Art Nouveau is a style found in the art, craft and design of the turn of the 20th century. Its motifs were often based on plants and flowers. In drawing, look at the work of Aubrey Beardsley (1872-1898); in interior design, at Charles Rennie Mackintosh (1868-1928); and in architecture, at the work of Antoni Gaudí (1852-1926).

BAROQUE

Baroque is a style of painting and sculpture which dominated European art (and architecture) during the 17th century; it is very complex and lively. There is often a feeling of movement in Baroque artworks which are also characterised by their symmetry. Well-known painters considered to have worked in the Baroque style include the Italian painter, Caravaggio (1573-1610) and the Dutch painter, Rembrandt (1606-1669).

Blaue Reiter

Blaue Reiter means 'Blue Rider' in German. It refers to a group of artists who adopted an abstract approach to Expressionism in their painting. The group includes Wassily Kandinsky (1866-1944), who founded the group in 1911, Franz Marc (1880-1916) and Paul Klee (1879-1940).

Brucke

Die Brucke means 'The Bridge' in German. It was the name taken by a group of Expressionist artists in 1905. Their work was influenced by artists such as van Gogh and the work of the Fauves. Their work was much more representational than that of the Blaue Reiter group. A leading exponent is Ernst Ludwig Kirchner (1880-1938).

Conceptual Art

Conceptual Art became prominent in the late 1960s, its main characteristic being a focus on the idea behind an artwork rather than the finished product. This means that the act of creating the artwork (or art event) is considered to be of more importance, and therefore of greater value, than what is finally created. In this way, it undermines the commercial aspect of art to which most Conceptual artists are opposed. Conceptual artists include Victor Burgin (1941-), Joseph Kosuth (1945-) and Sol LeWitt (1928-). Challenging the notion of art as a commodity (something which can be bought and sold) can be traced back to the Dada movement.

Concrete Art

This is nothing to do with using concrete as a medium! It is a kind of abstract art which has no reference at all to representation, and is concerned with pure form. The term was first used in this way by the painter Theo van Doesburg (1883-1931). It is not a coherent movement as such, more a style of art first conceived in the early part of the 20th century.

Cubism

Cubism is a term that was first used in 1908 to describe the work of Georges Braque (1882-1963), who, together with Picasso (1881-1973) developed the style. This artistic style had three phases; the first was a development of Cézanne's ideas about painting from nature – that artists should look for the cone, the sphere and the cube in nature and base their work upon those elements. The

'Cubism'

second phase is called analytical Cubism and is characterised by an emphasis on geometric shapes, with one viewpoint superimposed upon another. The third phase is called synthetic Cubism; this phase is characterised by the addition of collage.

Dadaism

The Dada movement was started around 1915/16 in Zurich by a French writer Tristan Tzara and artist Hans Arp (1887-1966). Tzara named the group by opening a French dictionary at random and finding the word *dada*, which is a child's word for a hobbyhorse.

Randomness and chance were key aspects to the work of the Dadaist artists, but their main aim was to question everything which was called art and to challenge middle-class values. Perhaps their most influential member was Marcel Duchamp (1887-1968) who will be remembered for (amongst other things) exhibiting a porcelain urinal entitled *Fountain*. Many of the ideas associated with the Dadaists continue to influence contemporary artists, particularly Conceptualists.

Expressionism

Expressionist artists attempt to convey emotions through their exaggerated use of colour and form. Expressionism describes art forms which put aside established rules for the use of colour, proportion, etc in favour of expressive and emotional qualities.

'Expressionism'

Early individual exponents of this approach to painting are Hieronymus Bosch (c1450-1516) and Matthias Grünewald (c1475-1528); other later pioneers include Georges Roualt (1871-1958) and Vincent van Gogh (1853-1890). German artists working in the first part of the 20th century formed a more coherent movement, with smaller groups developing their own styles, such as die Brucke,

Blaue Reiter, and Neue Sachlichkeit groups. Look also at the work of the Norwegian artist Edvard Munch (1863-1944).

Fauvism

Upon seeing a traditional sculpture surrounded by paintings with violent and crude colours at an exhibition in 1905, a French art critic remarked that the sculpture stood out like a Donatello (a Classical sculptor) amongst wild beasts ('fauves').

Fauvism is a term applied to a group of painters who used bold, clashing and unnatural colours in their work. Fauvist paintings are emotionally charged with very expressive brushwork.

Painters closely linked with this style are Henri Matisse (1869-1954), André Derain (1880-1954) and Maurice de Vlaminck (1876-1958).

Futurism

Futurism was a movement which flourished mainly between 1909 and 1915 in Italy, founded by the poet Marinetti. Futurists were sympathetic to the Italian Fascists and greatly admired all things modern: speed, energy, power, technology and machines. They wanted to capture in an original way the dynamism of the modern world, and reacted against what they saw as the dead, static art of their day. Futurist artists include Umberto Boccioni (1882-1916), Giacomo Balla (1871-1958) and Gino Severini (1883-1966).

Genre

Genre has two meanings: its general meaning refers simply to a type of painting, such as landscape, still life or abstract; its more specific meaning refers to the portrayal of everyday life in a painting, such as domestic interiors. It was the main art form in 17th-century Holland and is typified by the work of Jan Vermeer (1632-1675).

Impressionism

Impressionism is the term given to a movement of late 19th-century French artists whose major concern was with the effect of light. To achieve the right effects in their paintings, Impressionists would often paint out of doors rather than in a studio – this is known as 'plein air' painting. Their work is

'Impressionism'

characterised by everyday subject matter and the loose quality of the brushwork. Paint was often applied in separate strokes of pure colour – an approach which became fully developed in pointillism (see Neo-Impressionism on pages 28 and 29). Prominent Impressionist painters include Claude Monet (1840-1926), Camille Pissarro (1830-1903), Edouard Manet (1832-1883) and Pierre Auguste Renoir (1841-1919).

Installation Art

Installation Art is a contemporary art form which is related to and developed from Conceptual Art. Installation artists sometimes work anonymously (as a reaction against the notion of the artist being 'special'). Mixed media installations are 'installed' in both art galleries and non-art spaces and often aim to challenge ideas about what art is and who produces it. See the work of Mona Hartoum (1952-) as an example of a contemporary artist working in this way.

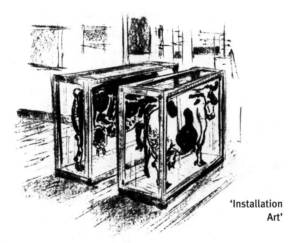

'Installation
Art'

Mannerism

Mannerism is a term applied to an artistic style which developed in Italy in the 16th century. It reacted against the balance and harmony which was typical of much Renaissance art, by using exaggeration and distortion in paintings. It was much more expressive than previous art forms. El Greco (1541-1614) and Tintoretto (1518-1594) are considered to be major Mannerist painters; some of Michelangelo's later sculptures have Mannerist qualities.

MODERN ART

Much of the art of the first half of the 20th century can be called 'Modern'. It is characterised by a concern for new ways of representation and the use of new materials. Modernism was essentially rebelling against anything which had gone before; eventually, once Modern Art became established, there was a need to rebel against itself – resulting in Post-Modernism. Modern Art should not be confused with contemporary art (see page 18).

NEO-CLASSICISM/ CLASSICAL

'Classical'

Classical art is characterised by harmony and balance; it is rational and controlled and keeps to well-defined rules. Its origins lie in Greek art of 400 BC, reaching its peak in 5th-century Greece. It flourished as Neo-Classicism in the rest of Europe in the 18th and 19th centuries. Classical art is often contrasted with Romantic art. The painter David (1748-1825) and the sculptor Antonio Canova (1757-1822) are examples of Neo-Classicists.

Neo-Impressionism

Neo-Impressionism means 'New' Impressionism – usually referring to work by Georges Seurat (1859-1891) and Paul Signac (1863-1935) who experimented with colour, characterised by the use of 'optical mixing', where colours placed next to each other on the canvas are blended by the eye. For example, dabs of blue paint placed next to dabs of red paint would appear from a distance to blend into violet. This approach to painting is also called 'divisionism' and 'pointillism'.

Neue Sachlichkeit

Sometimes called 'New Objectivity', this was a branch of German Expressionism which was more concerned with social comment than the artist's emotions. It is characterised by a concern for detail and exaggerated representation. Look at the work of Otto Dix (1891-1969) and George Grosz (1893-1959) for typical examples.

Op Art

Op Art stands for 'optical art' and is an art form based on abstract geometric patterns, usually lines, circles and squares, painted in strongly contrasting colours. The effect of such pictures is that they produce optical shimmers, flickering and after-images in the eye of the spectator. It flourished in the 1960s. Bridget Riley (1931-) and Victor Vasarely (1908-1997) are leading exponents of this style.

Photorealism

Sometimes called 'Superrealism' or 'Hyperrealism', this is a type of art which started in the 1960s and aimed to reproduce photographic reality in paintings and sculptures. The resulting work is often so skilfully produced that it is impossible to tell if the painting is a photograph or not. See the work of Chuck Close (1940-).

Pop Art

Pop Art refers to works of art which make use of images from popular culture, such as food labels and other mass-produced items. It emerged in the 1950s. Many examples of Pop Art are larger-scale versions of everyday objects, such as Andy Warhol's (1931-1987) soup can and Roy Lichtenstein's (1923-) paintings of comic strips.

'Pop Art'

Post-Impressionism

The term Post-Impressionism is usually applied to the work of Paul Cézanne (1839-1906), Vincent van Gogh (1853-1890) and Paul Gauguin (1848-1903). These three painters were not closely linked in terms of style, but were influenced by, and developed their own styles from, the Impressionist painters who preceded them.

POST-MODERNISM

Post-Modernism refers to a style or approach, particularly in architecture, which self-consciously combines a range of different styles. Look, for example, at the Clore Gallery at the Tate Britain by James Stirling (1926-1992). The work of a couple of British artists, Michael Baldwin (1945-) and Mel Ramsden (1944-), who together are called 'Art and Language', is considered to be Post-Modern, in that it refers to past styles and is heavily influenced by current ideas about art and society.

Pre-Raphaelite Art

The Pre-Raphaelite artists were formed in 1848 by a group of English artists, notably William Holman Hunt (1827-1910), John Everett Millais (1829-1896) (not to be confused with the French Impressionist painter Millet) and Dante Gabriel Rossetti (1828-1882). Their 'Brotherhood' wanted to produce a kind of art which they felt existed before Raphael (1483-1520) and they therefore held Medieval art in high esteem. Their work combined a Romantic idealism with a detailed naturalism. Their paintings were often concerned with Biblical, Shakespearean or Arthurian themes and told a moral story, often with elaborate symbolism. Pre-Raphaelite paintings were mostly painted directly from live models and real objects rather than from the imagination. They are characterised by vivid colours and attention to detail.

Realism

As an art movement, Realism refers to the social realism of 19th-century painters like Gustave Courbet (1819-1877) and Honoré Daumier (1808-1879).

'Realism'

They preferred to paint non-idealised versions of the world, including depictions of poverty and ordinary life. In a more general sense, realism refers to a type of art which attempts to recreate the world as it appears to be, without distortion of stylisation. In this sense, it is less ambiguous to use the term 'naturalism'.

RENAISSANCE

The word *renaissance* means rebirth – it refers to a period of time when art and science were felt to be reborn in the spirit of an earlier, Classical period. It began in Italy, particularly Florence, in around 1400 and spread to most of Europe throughout the 16th and 17th centuries. In England, it is said to have lasted into the 18th century.

Important developments in this period were: the use of oil paint; the introduction of linear and aerial perspective; and the development of anatomy and naturalism.

'Renaissance'

Significant artists, of which there are many associated with this period, are Michelangelo Buonarroti (1475-1564), Leonardo da Vinci (1452-1519), Sandro Botticelli (1445-1510), Albrecht Dürer (1471-1528) and Raphael Sanzio (1483-1520).

The reproductions on
these pages are provided
for you to examine some
famous artworks further.
You should also try to look
at some original artworks.

Anti-clockwise from top: *Woman in Profile* by Leonardo da Vinci; *The Milkmaid* by Jan Vermeer; *Mater Dolorosa* by El Greco.

Clockwise from top left: *Bar at the Folies-Bergères* by Edouard Manet; *Portrait of Dr Gachet* by Vincent van Gogh; Paul Cézanne's *The Card Players*.

From top: *Birth* by
Jackson Pollock;
Glass on a Table by
Georges Braque.

From top: Salvador Dali's *Metamorphosis of Narcissus*;
Whaam! by Roy Lichtenstein.

Rococo

Rococo is a highly ornamental style of art and design which was popular in 18th-century France, particularly during the period 1735 to 1745 during the reign of Louis XV. The style was a reaction to Baroque and was characterised by its more dainty, delicate motifs in the form of rocks, shells and foliage. Artists of this time include Antoine Watteau (1684-1721) and Jean Honoré Fragonard (1732-1806).

ROMANTICISM

Romanticism was a movement which rebelled against the formality and rationality of Classicism. Although it was most prominent as an approach to art in the 18th and 19th centuries, its emphasis on imagination, expression and individual creativity is still prominent in the art of today. Romantics include Joseph Turner (1775-1851) and Eugène Delacroix (1798-1863).

'Romanticism'

Site-Specific Art

Site-Specific Art is artwork that has been made especially for a certain place, and makes use of the visual aspects of that place. An example is *Two Levels* by Daniel Buren (1938-). This is a sculptural installation created specifically for the Cour d'Honneur of the Palais Royal in Paris in 1985-6. More information on Site-Specific Art is provided on pages 43 to 45.

'Site-Specific Art'

Surrealism

Surrealism was an artistic movement which was started in France by a poet, André Breton, in 1924. It was influenced by the then new study of psychology and sought to represent the subconscious world of dreams and visions.

'Surrealism'

Surrealist art is characterised by the juxtaposition of things and ideas which are not normally associated. Although as an art movement it lasted from the 1920s to the 1960s, it still influences many artists, and continues to be popular with young people as a way of expressing their thoughts and feelings. See the work of Salvador Dali (1904-1989), René Magritte (1898-1967) and Giorgio de Chirico (1888-1978).

Vorticism

This was an abstract art movement which was influenced by both Cubism and Futurism. It was founded by the British artist and writer Wyndham Lewis (1882-1957) in 1913. The sculptors Henri Gaudier-Brzeska (1891-1915) and Jacob Epstein (1880-1959) are associated with it.

Hopefully, this section will help you use ideas from art movements in your own work. It is important for you to be able to show that you know the influences from which you have drawn inspiration. Bear in mind, however, that being influenced by an artist or art movement is not the same as copying, or producing a pastiche.

Lists such as the one above tend to be overwhelmingly 'Western'. It would take several books to cover the art of other cultures in the same detail. We cannot, for example, simply talk about 'African' art since Africa is a continent which contains approximately fifty very different countries with huge variations in culture. You should ensure that you find out about non-Western styles of art as well.

A print by the Japenese artist Ando Hiroshige (1797-1858)

There are of course thousands of different styles and approaches to art-making from different cultures throughout history. The following are a few suggestions for you to begin your exploration of other art forms:

- contemporary pottery from the Yorubu people of Nigeria
- contemporary textiles from the Bambara people of Mali
- Islamic ceramics from North African countries such as Morocco, Tunisia and Algeria
- bronzework from 16th-century Benin
- miniature painting from the Mughal Empire (India) between the 16th and 18th centuries
- Japanese prints from the Edo period (1603-1868).

You might also want to look at Russian folk art, Chinese watercolour painting, Pre-Columbian pottery from Latin America – the list is virtually endless!

Art in context

When looking at art, thinking about the context of the work (ie the time, place and circumstances in which it was made) will help you understand why an artist produced work in a particular way.

A First World War artist in the trenches

You will sometimes hear of the term 'contextual studies'. This refers to understanding the different contexts in which art is or has been produced.

Contexts can be:

- **Social** – What was happening in society at the time?
- **Technological** – What materials and equipment were available to the artist?
- **Cultural** – What, for example, was the dominant religion and how did this affect customs?
- **Historical** – What had gone before? What had not yet happened?

No artist works in isolation; all are influenced by their environment, whether that environment is other artists, television, or the built environment surrounding them. All artists also produce their artwork according to how they believe art should be produced, eg whether it is concerned with social comment, beauty, realism or expression.

Site-Specific Art

Certain art styles and movements have more in common with the context in which *you* are working – at the beginning of the 21st century in a technologically advanced, multi-cultural society – than others. One such art style is Site-Specific Art.

As defined in the previous section, Site-Specific Art is artwork that has been made especially for a certain place. It can make you look at a familiar place in a completely different way.

The same is true if the artist places an everyday object in an art gallery. It makes you think 'Why has the artist put this here? What was their intention?' You could come across Site-Specific Art absolutely anywhere in your everyday life... walking down the street, in a tube station, in a library or on the bus.

The materials that artists use to make artwork for a specific place are very varied and range from natural materials like leaves, to found objects, to photography, painting and sculpture.

Often, artists use a combination of materials within the work, for example, found objects and photographs. When you use more than one kind of material in a work, it is described as mixed media.

In Site-Specific Art, the boundaries between what is art and what is life become blurred. The site (for example, the tube station, bus or art gallery) has significance and becomes part of the artwork. The artwork only exists because of its relationship to the chosen site. This type of art-making is sometimes associated with Installation Art. Often, artists use installations in public places to get people thinking and talking about contemporary issues. This could be anything from environmental issues, to social issues such as homelessness, to debates about art itself.

The Angel of the North by Anthony Gormley is an example of Site-Specific Art, situated near Gateshead

The *context* of the work gives it its meaning.

Creating your own Site-Specific Art

You can create your own Site-Specific Art anywhere, even your own bedroom. One idea is to think about your school as the starting point for making a piece of artwork. Using some of the following strategies, you could develop a piece of artwork to be displayed within a place that you have chosen in the school grounds.

Go on a walk around the school and find places that interest you. Use a camera (perhaps a digital camera) to record your walk around the school. Take photographs of the places that interest you.

To study a site in detail, it is useful to make observational drawings and written notes. How does the site make you feel? Perhaps you could play a word game with a friend – try and think of all the words that you associate with a place. Keep going as long as you can until you begin to repeat one or more of the words. Make a note of these words.

What is the history of your school? The school library will be a good starting point in researching the history of the school. Can you find any old school photographs? What stories can you gather?

These starting points should help you uncover lots of interesting material from which to develop an art project. Choose the site that interests you the most and think about why it interests you. What could you make and put in that site that would interest other people? What would get them to look at a familiar place within the school in a new way?

Art and culture

As part of your course, you will be expected to show your understanding of how art, craft and design contribute and relate to different areas of human experience. Some background information about the spiritual, moral, social and cultural aspects of art is given in this section.

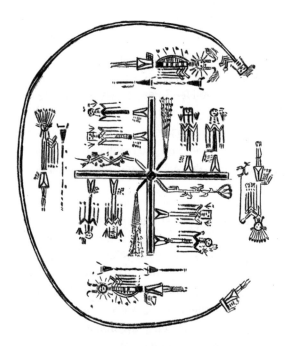

American Indian spiritual work such as this is produced during ritualistic ceremonies

Spiritual aspects

Traditionally, art has been a means of depicting religious experience, for example, in the work of Medieval artists and craftworkers in Christian architecture, and the Islamic designs found in mosques.

You might find it rewarding to visit a Christian cathedral – they were designed and constructed to fill people with a sense of awe and wonder. You might also find it useful to look at Tantric art, which is associated with Hinduism.

However, spirituality in art is not confined to religion. Both Wassily Kandinsky (1866-1944) and Piet Mondrian (1872-1944) tried to have a spiritual dimension to their paintings. Kandinsky wrote extensively about spirituality in art, as well as producing paintings; Mondrian tried to portray, amongst other things, the essence of harmony through the careful use of colour and balance in his compositions.

Moral aspects

Some artists have intentionally focused on the moral aspect of life and have tried to tell a particular story through their work. For example, the paintings of the Pre-Raphaelite artist William Holman Hunt (1827-1910) are often full of symbolism which is intended to make a moral point.

Find a reproduction of a painting by Holman Hunt (or better still, go and see an original in the Tate Modern or Birmingham City Art Gallery), and see what you can find out about it. Look also at the engravings of William Hogarth (1697-1764).

The Garden of Earthly Delights, by Hieronymus Bosch (c1450-1516) is an example of a moralistic work. Find a reproduction of it and then try to find out what you think it is about, using the 4R approach described on pages 11 to 13.

Social issues

Many artists and designers have been concerned with commenting upon society in their work, such as the Social Realists (part of the Realist movement). A lot of contemporary art is concerned with social comment, such as the status of women in society – see, for example, the work of Cindy Sherman (1954-).

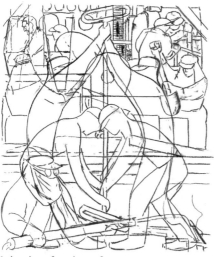

Some artists, such as Diego Rivera (1886-1957), have produced work of a political nature in the form of murals.

Designers and craftspeople have also been aware of social issues. For example, William Morris (1834-1896) attempted to link his work with his social ideas, defining art as 'man's expression of his joy in labour'.

A drawing of workers after (ie influenced by) Diego Rivera

Find out what you can about William Morris and the Arts and Crafts movement. For further reading on the social aspect of designing, see Victor Papanek's *Design for the Real World*, and *The Green Imperative*. Although they are aimed at older students, you should hopefully find them interesting; they are concerned with prompting a greater social awareness among designers and consumers.

Designers are often expected by manufacturers to design things which are useful and/or beautiful, but which are cheap to produce. Consider the effects which certain products, such as plastic novelties, hardwood furniture and motor cars, have on the environment; consider also the pay and conditions of workers around the world who are involved in the production of designed goods.

Cultural aspects

Think about the nature of your cultural heritage and where you can find visual examples of it. Museums and galleries are the obvious places to start but you can find visual examples of culture all around you – on packaging and advertisements, on book and CD covers, clothes, tattoos, furniture, fabrics – in fact, everywhere you

UK 1960s-style chair design

look. Look particularly at your built environment and try to find out the architectural styles of buildings; find out when they were built and what artists were around at that time.

To find out about different cultures, you can visit not only museums, but also religious buildings, such as synagogues, churches, temples and mosques. Look at the kind of decoration that can be found on the walls in these buildings. How do they differ from that of your own culture? What things are similar?

16th-century
Islamic tile

Some things mean different things in different cultures and at different times. The colour green, for example, has meant both hope and jealousy in Western culture, but now is more likely to stand for something to do with the environment.

In *The Arnolfini Marriage*, a painting from 1434 by Jan van Eyck (which can be found in the National Gallery in London), there is a dog which is said to represent faithfulness in the marriage. However, in Islamic culture, a picture of a dog would never be found in such a painting because dogs are considered to be unclean.

Furthermore, in Islamic culture, it is forbidden to represent the full form of an animal or human, especially in a religious context. There are several reasons for this, including the need to avoid idol worship, and the fact that the maker of an image is sometimes seen as competing with God and eventually will be expected to give it life (according to Islamic culture).

Try to find out about the following symbols and how they vary between cultures:

- Dragons – are they wise or evil?
- The colour red – is it dangerous or lucky?
- The swastika – where was it used before the Nazis?
- A wavy line – has it the same meaning on a street sign as it has in Australian Aboriginal art?

Being creative

Being creative is not just about 'creating things'; it is also a way of thinking and an approach to solving problems. Art is well-placed to develop your creative and imaginative responses.

What makes a particular response creative? Originality is one thing, but not the only thing. Ripping up your art examination paper might be an original response, but it is not creative, because it is not a *suitable* response. You need to invest some time, thought and skill into your work in order to respond to problems creatively. You could think of creativity in terms of a simple equation:

Originality + Quality + Suitability = Creativity

Practice exercises for thinking creatively

The following tasks (which are similar to those found in 'creativity tests') should help stimulate your mind to start thinking creatively:

- Design a machine to weigh an elephant.

- Invent a sleep machine.

- How would you build a house quickly?

How would you weigh an elephant?

- How would you improve the human body?
- Design a machine for carrying a person to the centre of the Earth.
- Add to the shapes below.

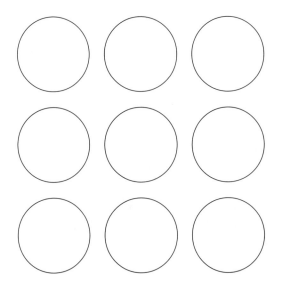

There are no 'right' or 'wrong' answers to any of the above tasks. You should, however, try to think about how you could judge the outcomes. You could do them together with a group of friends and perhaps discuss the results and vote for the most creative solution.

How many of you drew *outside* the circles in the final task? Being creative requires the confidence to break out of established ways of doing things. This is something which can be achieved with practice and a willingness to experiment.

Experimenting with drawing

It is important for you to develop your confidence and try a range of different techniques, approaches and materials. For example, drawing does not only mean using a pencil on a piece of white paper; you can draw with almost anything that will make a mark, upon anything that will receive it. Drawing does not have to be *of* something (like a flower); it can also be *about* something (such as movement).

A drawing of movement

Working with a friend

- Draw each other's head without looking at the board/paper.

- Draw onto the head using the opposite hand to usual.

- Draw onto the head without taking your pencil off the surface of the paper or board.

- Begin with a scribble and pass it to your partner for a response. They should make a mark or line in relation to what is already there. Continue to do this until the paper is full.

Depicting movement

Arrange a group of up to 12 assorted objects on a table. Make a coloured drawing, from above, of the objects in this position. Then move the objects slightly to new positions. Add to the drawing in a different colour, to record the new position. Repeat again using a different colour. Consider speed, rhythm, weight; think of the drawing as a kind of 'dance'.

Working from non-visual sources

Draw an image for the sounds produced by a whistle, a radio or a mouth-organ, for example, or screaming and shouting, clapping, animal noises, percussion instruments, or scraping.

A picture of sound

Depicting feelings

Instead of drawing from observation, try drawing by feeling – put an object in a bag and record what you feel.

Experimenting with space

Paper comes in standard sizes (eg A4, A3, A2, A1) – A4 is the size you usually find in photocopiers and is used for letters; A3 is twice that; A2 is twice A3; A1 is twice A2 and is the largest size. Consider working on totally different sizes (and shapes). To release your imagination, free you from old habits, and break conventions, try:

Record a landscape at postage stamp size

- recording a landscape at postage stamp size

- working with (removable) chalk on a school playground or other large hard surfaces

- using two sheets of A1 stuck together for a self-portrait.

Draw a huge self-portrait

Materials and techniques

A rt can be created from almost anything, but here are a few hints about some of the more commonly-used materials, as well as some tips on selected approaches to making art. Further information on various materials and techniques can be found in the glossary on page 93.

An example page from a sketchbook

Sketchbooks

Sketchbooks are extremely useful for jotting down ideas and recording visual information. This is essential to the process of art-making; most artists will have a sketchbook or a notebook of some kind. Information can be in any form, such as scraps of patterned paper, bus tickets, poems or quick sketches of incidents you see on your way to and from school. You can use your sketchbook as a kind of visual diary. Its most important function though is as a record of your research.

A sketchbook will help you to develop:

- a personal, individual style
- confidence, and the freedom to make mistakes
- an ability to think about your work.

Pencils

The pencil is perhaps your most useful drawing tool, but you should use the appropriate pencil for your needs. The 'lead' of pencils is actually graphite, which comes in varying degrees of softness. Most pencils in everyday use have HB written on them – this stands for Hard Black.

Hard pencils sometimes have F written on their side (standing for Fine); or from H through to 6H – these pencils are suited to very precise technical drawing.

Use the appropriate pencil for your needs

Softer pencils go from B through to 6B or even softer; they are good for sketching where large areas of dark shading are needed. You would probably only need a small selection, such as one HB, one 2B and one 6B pencil. Keep your pencils very sharp. When drawing, you can vary both the pressure (by pressing down hard or lightly according to the effect you want) and the angle at which the pencil is held relative to the paper.

Paper

There is a huge choice of paper and so it is important to choose the kind most suitable for your needs. You should consider the nature of the paper:

- Do you need it to be rough or smooth?
- Does it need to be coloured or plain white? What kind of white?
- How big do you want it?
- What shape do you want it?

Paper quality is important:

Watercolour paper is expensive paper, which is usually thick and textured. It is meant for liberal applications of watery paint.

Art paper has a smooth surface and is suitable for fine pen and ink drawing.

Tinted paper gives good effects with pastels, as does brown wrapping paper; paper with a rough fibrous quality is better for pastels to stick to.

Try using **old newspapers** with pen and ink or wax crayons – the print and photographs add to the tone qualities you can achieve.

You could experiment with all kinds of surfaces – for example, dried leaves.

Drawing

The best way to learn to improve your drawing skill is by drawing from observation. When beginning a drawing, plan it out by drawing extremely lightly, with hardly any pressure, so that you have a general idea of the size and shape of your subject on the paper. Then continue to put in more and more lines very lightly to act as reference points. When you are confident that you have the right proportions, you can begin to apply more pressure.

Look very carefully at the negative spaces as well as the positive spaces. If you are drawing a chair, for example, look at the spaces between the legs as well as the legs themselves. Half-close your eyes and look through your eyelashes to see the areas of light and dark.

In general, try to make lines which are 'nearer' to you bolder, by applying slightly more pressure.

Linear perspective

Linear perspective projection is a very good system for creating the effect of depth and distance in a drawing. There are at least three kinds of linear perspective –

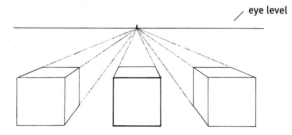

One point perspective – the lines converge on one point

one point, two point and three point – and they each
follow the same rules. The main rule is that all lines
converge on one or more vanishing points.

In one and two point perspective, the vanishing
points are always at eye level, on an imaginary
horizon, and depend on the height the viewer is
from the ground. Try crouching down and then
standing on a chair, noting how your view of the
world changes and particularly how the horizon
moves up and down.

Try drawing directly onto a picture of a room
interior in an old magazine – draw lines along all of
the surfaces and edges and find out where the eye
level and vanishing points are.

In a one point perspective drawing, all of the 'depth
lines' go to one vanishing point; in two point
perspective, there are two vanishing points on the
eye level. In three point perspective, the third
vanishing point is above or below the eye level.

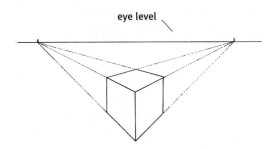

Two point perspective – the lines converge on two points

Paint

Many people associate art with paintings –
paintings are made by using paint, but what is
paint? Paint is made from three main things:

- a pigment, which gives it colour
- a medium to support the pigment
- a thinning agent.

There are a number of different types of paint you
can use, which will give you very different results:

Oil paint is made from pigments mixed with oils,
and can be thinned with turpentine or linseed oil. It
takes a long time to dry and can be applied very
thickly (often with a knife instead of a brush).

Acrylic paint can be used thickly or watered down.
It dries very quickly and, once dry, it is waterproof.

Watercolour paint is mixed with water and is
usually applied in translucent washes (ie the paper
can be seen through it).

Other types of paint include gouache, which is a
thick water-based paint, and tempera, which is
made from egg.

Canvas

Canvas is a common material for painting upon,
especially with oil paint (although many artists
prefer to use board).

Canvas has to be prepared by stretching it over a wooden frame and then priming it. This can be done by painting on two coats of acrylic primer (white emulsion paint is acceptable). Canvas and other absorbent materials are primed so that they can more readily accept paint; a primed surface gives the right amount of absorbency and provides a consistent white surface.

Printmaking

There are several different types of printmaking processes. The most commonly used broad classifications are: relief, intaglio, and monoprints.

A printmaker at work in her studio

Relief printing

Relief printing can include what are sometimes called linoprints or linocuts, as well as any form of printing where the image is taken from the surface. In linoprinting, you cut away areas from the surface; the parts which are left are the areas which will be printed after printing ink has been applied (usually with a roller).

Intaglio prints

This is a term used to describe prints which come from below the surface, as opposed to a relief print. Here, it is the parts of the surface you remove which will be printed.

Monoprints

Monotype prints are one-off prints – they are very quick and easy to do. Simply ink up a tile using a roller, and lightly place paper over the top of the inked tile without applying any pressure to the surface. Draw onto the back of the paper using a cocktail stick or something similar (or even a pencil). It might be helpful to rest your arm on a pile of books to keep it steady and to stop it touching the paper and pressing on the surface. Then peel off the paper to reveal what you have drawn.

Another type of printmaking process used by artists is **screen printing**. Ink is squeezed through a 'screen' (a fine mesh) onto paper to produce the print. The image which is created on the screen (also known as the stencil) prevents ink from passing through it and so appears on the paper as an uninked area.

Monoprints – what you draw...   ... appears printed in reverse

3-D art

The most well-known forms of 3-D art are sculpture and modelling in such materials as marble and bronze, but you can create 3-D artwork from any kind of media, from leather to ceramics.

Many sculptures start off as a kind of skeleton, called an armature. An armature is the framework around which a clay, plaster, paper or soft sculpture is moulded.

When constructing an armature, think about how big you want the sculpture to be (its scale), how heavy it will be (its weight) and how it will balance. You could produce a trial model of the sculpture on a smaller scale (known as a maquette) first to see how it will work.

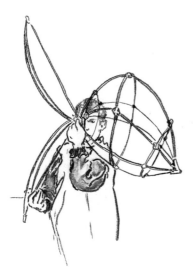

An armature for a fish made from withies
(flexible willow sticks) and masking tape

You can construct armatures out of almost anything, including chicken wire, card and wire. Be resourceful – milk cartons, coat hangers, tin cans, blown-up balloons and cardboard boxes are some examples of materials that you can use in three-dimensional work in imaginative ways. Here are a few ideas:

Chicken wire is a lightweight wire mesh that can be used to make basic shapes for a sculpture. Wire can also be used to join other materials to chicken wire to construct larger-scale sculptures. You can cut, bend and twist wire into any shape you can imagine and to give a sculpture movement.

Card is a useful material which can be bent, folded, scored, cut and ripped. You can roll cardboard into cylinders to form legs.

Papier mâché consists of paper mixed with glue, and is a fantastic medium for covering large lightweight structures like an armature made of chicken wire. It is also effective for modelling over hollow shapes such as inflated balloons. When dry, papier mâché can be painted or varnished.

Paper pulp offers you a different range of surface textures to papier mâché, and can be modelled on top of card and wire armatures. It is a very tactile material that you can push, press, mould, indent, pinch, squeeze, impress and layer over an armature. You can smooth the surface or experiment with different surface textures. A rough texture can be very effective, especially when lit because of the shadows created on the surface.

Plaster of Paris is a white powder that, when mixed with water, heats up and sets rock hard in about ten minutes. Plaster has many properties which make it excellent for modelling and also for carving. Once the plaster is dry, you can carve back into it using a knife or improvise with a variety of tools to achieve different surface textures – for example, a file to smooth the surface or a nail to scratch into it.

You can also model with soft materials, such as fabric, felt, plastic, latex, hessian, foam, cloth and wool. Think about the qualities of the soft material (for example, how 'stretchy' it is) and consider what you can do with it. How can you use these materials in a sculpture? You can stiffen, squash, cut, rip, wrinkle, crease, fill, soften, stretch, cover, weave, hang or crunch them!

Clay

Clay occurs naturally in the earth. It is dug up and purified before use. It is a very useful medium as it can be easily moulded or modelled. To make a clay model or pot permanent, it needs to be heated in a kiln to a very high temperature so that it undergoes a chemical change. Once 'fired' in this way, it cannot be made soft again.

It is important that there are no air bubbles in the clay as this will make the piece explode in the kiln. The clay should be 'wedged' (pounded) before you start to remove any air.

After firing, the piece can then be glazed (made shiny). This involves giving it a special coating and a further firing in the kiln.

Carving

Many different materials can be used for carving, for example, wood, stone and ice. Soap is a good material to use when you first start carving as it is cheap and easy to work with.

You could try carving out of ice

To get some ideas for your carving you could research different cultures and artists that use carving. Some examples you could look at are traditional masks from some African countries (often carved from wood) and the traditional work of Maoris, who live in New Zealand – they created beautiful wood carvings to decorate their homes. See if you can find any more examples of sculptors who use carving as their method of creating sculptures.

Colour

Have you ever tried to mix a colour and you couldn't get it right? You might know that red and blue make violet or purple, but sometimes when you try it, all you get is a reddish-brown colour.

This is because there are different kinds of reds and different kinds of blues. It is important to be aware of the actual name of the colour you are using. For example, if you mix cadmium red with

Abstract art often uses colour to great effect

cerulean blue, you are likely to end up with a brown rather than a violet colour; the best violet can be obtained by mixing alizarin crimson and ultramarine blue. You should experiment as much as you can with different colours – be bold and build up your confidence; not every effort has to be a finished masterpiece!

Hue, saturation and tone

Colours have three aspects: hue, saturation and tone.

Hue

Hue refers to the 'yellowness', 'redness' or 'blueness' of a colour. For example, the difference between scarlet and crimson is one of hue; crimson has more 'blue', whereas scarlet has more 'yellow'.

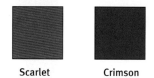

Scarlet　　　Crimson

There are about 150 perceptible differences of hue. When using pigment, such as oil paint or watercolour, the three traditional artists' primary hues are yellow, red and blue; these cannot be mixed from other colours. Secondary hues in the artists' palette are green, orange and violet; these can be mixed using primary colours.

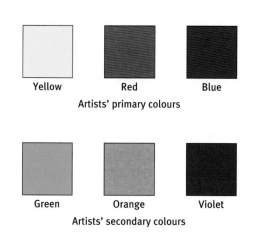

Yellow　　　Red　　　Blue

Artists' primary colours

Green　　　Orange　　　Violet

Artists' secondary colours

In commercial printing, the primary colours are instead cyan, magenta and yellow. Black is also used to strengthen darker colours. This is known as 4-colour process printing or CMYK.

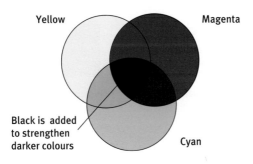

Colours used in 4-colour process printing

When working with coloured light (for example, on a TV screen or computer monitor), the primary hues are blue, red and green. When added together, they make white. These primary hues of physics should not be confused with the primary hues of artists' pigments.

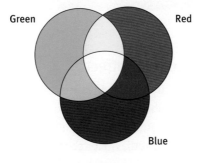

Primary colours of light

Saturation

Saturation refers to the purity of a colour and is often used in the same way as intensity or, occasionally, brilliance. A really deep, rich colour is said to be highly saturated.

Saturated red   Non-saturated red

Tone

Tone refers to differences in the lightness or darkness of a hue. *Tint* is the usual term for a light hue, being a colour to which white has been added. *Shade* usually refers to dark hues where black has been added.

Shade   Tint

Using colour for effect

Some colours are said to advance (that is, come towards you), while others are said to recede (go away from you). Advancing colours are usually 'warm' (ie mainly red), while receding colours are usually 'cool' (mainly blue). In addition, saturated colours tend to advance while less saturated colours tend to recede.

The saturated red and green advance more than the less saturated blue

Abstract artists can make use of this to create an illusion of space and depth. Advancing and receding colours can also be used in landscape painting where an effect of distance is desired. This is called aerial or atmospheric perspective. The effect of distance can be achieved by using cooler and less saturated colours, which are often also paler in tone; this can be done very simply by thinning down the paint (with water if it is water-based, such as gouache and acrylic; or white spirit if it is oil paint).

A colour wheel

Your teacher might sometimes refer to a colour wheel. This can be used to show relationships between colours. Typically, colours on the right side of the wheel are 'warm', whereas colours on the left side are 'cool'.

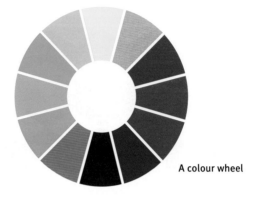

A colour wheel

Complementary colours are those which contrast with each other; in a 'colour wheel' they are opposite.

Analogous colours harmonise and are found next to each other in a colour wheel.

Placing two complementary colours next to each other will make them appear to increase in intensity. Adding one complementary colour to another (eg adding blue to orange) will result in a duller colour – the saturation will have been reduced.

Generally speaking, the more that colours are mixed with other colours, the duller they get. The Impressionist painters, particularly the Neo-Impressionists such as Seurat, used 'optical mixing' to achieve a fresher appearance. This involves placing, for example, blue and red specks of paint next to each other so that from a distance they appear violet.

ICT in art

ICT (Information and Communication Technology) in art is nowadays commonplace, and contemporary artists often use computers as an important tool.

There are numerous possibilities for using computers in artwork. Perhaps their most practical application is in testing out ideas, such as colour changes on designs. Creating repeating patterns also becomes extremely easy and far less time-consuming than when using traditional methods.

Creating repeating patterns is easy using ICT

Computers cannot do the work for you – they simply use the information you put in to create different effects.

To make the image on the right, the image on the left has been rotated and cropped, the colours manipulated and effects such as glows and sharpening applied

Images can be downloaded from the Internet, a CD-ROM or a digital camera, or scanned in. They can then be changed by adding elements (such as words or other images), taking things away (such as the background), manipulating colours and shapes (resizing, rotating, shearing, cropping, etc) or distorting (blurring, adding 'noise', etc) – there are several programs available which will allow you to do this.

The three images above have been combined to create the montage on the left

Images can also be created directly in a graphics, paint or illustration program using the mouse or a stylus (pen) on a graphics tablet.

Interesting effects can be created by combining traditional approaches to painting and drawing with images manipulated on the computer screen. Images can be printed out to be worked on further, using collage, photomontage, or just drawn on with a pen.

Here, a drawn portrait was scanned in and manipulated in a graphics package to make a Cubist portrait

There is a whole range of software available – for drawing, painting, manipulating photographs and other images, animation and 3-D design.

Images require a lot of memory for them to be stored in the computer and it is often necessary to use a zip drive to move them to another computer. There are currently two ways in which computers store images – either as *raster* graphics (where the image is held as a *bitmap*) or *vector* graphics.

Bitmap images are made up of a collection of tiny picture elements (which are like dots) called pixels. If the image is enlarged, the pixels are simply made bigger and, consequently, the image loses its sharpness. In vector graphics, images are stored as a series of instructions (in the form of an algorithm). Vector images can be enlarged without any loss of detail since every time the picture is enlarged, it is effectively redrawn. Vector graphics also take up less memory. Both bitmap and vector graphics software can be used to explore and experiment with visual elements of colour, shape, pattern, form, three-dimensional space and texture (see the glossary on page 93 for definitions of these elements).

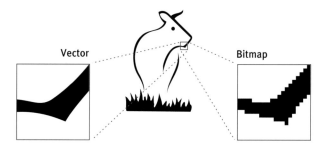

Images can either be stored as vector or bitmap images

It is important that you use ICT *appropriately*. This means only using it when the outcome is likely to be more interesting or of a better quality than you can achieve using traditional methods. For example, avoid using clip art (pre-prepared computer graphics), unless you intend to manipulate it in some way!

It is also a good idea to use ICT to the full when researching ideas for art, and when finding out about artists and art movements (eg searching the Internet or CD-ROMs, keeping word-processed notes, storing images). However, make sure that you carefully select, analyse and critically evaluate the material you find – that means not simply downloading information and presenting it as your own!

A very useful Web site which acts as a gateway to over 2500 museums, galleries and other similar places is the 24-hour museum at www.24hourmuseum.org.uk. You can browse the site for all the latest news and you can use the museum finder to search for art galleries and museums by the type of things they have on display, by their location, or by their name.

More and more people have Internet access these days, either at school or at home, and this access often comes with the facility to put up a Web page. This provides the perfect opportunity to have an exhibition of your own artwork on the World Wide Web.

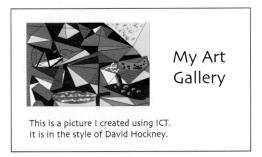

My Art Gallery

This is a picture I created using ICT.
It is in the style of David Hockney.

You can exhibit your artwork on the World Wide Web

National Curriculum requirements

The National Curriculum is a useful starting point for you to use in order to develop your skills and understanding of art and design. It provides a framework which you can build upon, although there is no reason why you cannot break a few rules – that is, after all, what artists have been doing for hundreds of years!

However, while at school, it is wise to know about, and normally to play by, the rules. The following gives a brief overview of what is expected and how you will be assessed. This should give you a good idea of what you need to do to gain a top grade in Art and Design.

The Attainment Target

There is one overall 'Attainment Target' for Art and Design, entitled *Knowledge, Skills and Understanding*. This means that, in your Art and Design lessons, you will be expected to do work which not only involves *creating* art but also *learning about* art. This Attainment Target is divided into four aspects:

- exploring and developing ideas
- investigating and making art, craft and design
- evaluating and developing work
- knowledge and understanding.

You will be expected to use a range of materials and approaches, including three-dimensional work and Information and Communication Technology (ICT), and to investigate the work of other artists, past and present, in order to inform your own art-making.

Assessment Levels

You will be assessed, as in other subject areas, according to Levels. In Art and Design, Assessment Levels are concerned with the areas outlined below:

- exploring and developing ideas – the extent to which you experiment with and use a range of materials and techniques to express ideas
- investigating and making – the extent to which you show your skills in exploring ideas through making art objects
- evaluating and developing work – how well you can reflect upon your work and make changes to it in the light of your judgements.

How much you *know* and *understand* about art helps you make progress in these three areas.

Level Descriptions provide the basis on which teachers make judgements about your performance at the end of each key stage. At Key Stage 4, national qualifications, such as GCSE, assess your attainment in Art and Design. Guidance on the GCSE examination in Art and Design is included on page 87.

The Level Descriptions all use similar words, but differ in terms of quality and quantity expected. For example, the first sentence in each Level Description states that students should:

Level 4:

> *'collect visual and other information'*

Level 8:

> *'evaluate relevant visual and other information, analysing how codes and conventions are used to represent ideas, beliefs and values in different genres, styles and traditions'*

Exceptional Performance (above Level 8):

> *'critically evaluate relevant visual and other information and make connections between representations in different genres, styles and traditions'*

There is a clear progression from 'collect visual information' at Level 4, to *'evaluate relevant* visual information' at Level 8, to *'critically* evaluate relevant visual information *and make connections'* in Exceptional Performance.

To give an example of the difference between the Levels, consider being asked to:

> *'Use the Internet to gather information about an artist.'*

A student working at Level 4 might look up the artist's name, download all of the information, sort out what looks the most interesting, and label it.

You can use the Internet to find out about an artist

Working at Level 8, you would be expected to ensure that the information you had was suitable for your needs. You would also need to show, by your presentation of the information, that you had carefully considered what to use and how to use it.

At the higher level of Exceptional Performance, your evaluation would need to be more thorough and well-considered. For example, you might use *your own words* to show that you understand the relationship between an artist's work and that of other artists (including your own).

It is a good idea, when undertaking any research, to look up all words that are unfamiliar to you. For instance, the French word *genre* means a particular type of painting, such as landscape, abstract or still life.

Other terms, eg *conventions*, may need more careful investigation. To give an example of conventions in art: in order to depict distance and depth in a picture, Chinese watercolourists would paint distant objects higher up in the picture; in Ancient Egypt, space was shown mainly by overlapping; in Renaissance times, much use was made of perspective to show depth and distance. All of these are different conventions.

Chinese watercolourists paint distant objects higher up in the picture

In Ancient Egypt, space was shown by overlapping

Key Skills

There are also a number of key skills which can be developed through art. These skills are:

- communication
- application of number
- Information Technology (IT)
- working with others
- improving own learning and performance
- problem solving.

Through exploring and recording ideas in your sketchbook, and by discussing starting points and source materials for your artwork, you can improve your **communication** skills.

You will also find it useful to evaluate your own and your friends' artwork, making use of an art-specific vocabulary whenever possible. It is important to talk about art, craft and design with others; you should reflect on your own and others' work and plan ways to develop your own work further.

If you 'scale-up' (ie make bigger through using a grid) your preparatory drawings for a larger-scale painting, you are applying an understanding of **number**. You can also demonstrate your numeracy skills through using patterns, shape and forms in two and three dimensions.

You can develop your **IT** skills through using the Internet to investigate the work of artists, craftspeople and designers, and by making use of a range of art and design-related software (see the section on ICT in art on page 75).

Through collaborating on large-scale projects, and responding to a design brief, you can show how you are able to **work with others** as part of a team.

The evaluating and developing work aspect of art and design, which involves thinking about your work, undertaking research and making changes to develop your artwork, will help you to **improve your learning and performance**.

Your skills in **problem solving** can be enhanced through manipulating materials, processes and technologies. You should experiment as much as possible, testing and adapting ideas and arriving at a range of different solutions using different art, craft and design processes.

GCSE Art and Design

The GCSE examination is meant to find out what you *can* do, not what you *cannot* do. In Art and Design, this is particularly important to bear in mind because, as this book tries to demonstrate, there are no 'right' or 'wrong' answers.

At GCSE, you will need to pay particular attention to using your sketchbook. Sketchbooks are not just for sketching! Use your sketchbook to stick down examples of colours and patterns. You could also include magazine articles of artists and designers who interest you, or examples of fashion and design which you find inspiring. Sketchbooks can also be used to make written notes, to jot down ideas and to experiment with different media.

The following information is grouped according to the 'assessment objectives' for GCSE Art and Design, in other words, areas upon which you will be marked: investigation, experimentation, documentation and presentation.

Include any items of interest in your sketchbook

Investigation

You should record things you see around you and experience as much as possible. Not only will your artistic skills steadily improve because of the practice, but you will also acquire the skill to record from your memory and imagination.

You should aim to do as much as possible from direct observation. Avoid using too much of what is often termed 'second-hand material'; in other words, copying from what other people have done (such as cartoons) and from photographs. It is certainly easier, for example, to copy a face from a photograph than it is to draw or paint from real life, but the results are often not as good. A drawing copied from a photograph often appears flat and lifeless in comparison.

Try to make use of other forms of recording, such as photography, modelling, animation and video.

The whole of what you see is at your disposal for you to investigate – not just looking at and recording what you see, but researching what is behind the things you see, and exploring why things are the way they are.

Experimentation

You need to show that you are capable of developing your work. This means showing that you can use a starting point, such as sketches of a building from observation, to explore aspects of visual form; you could look at structure, colour, or any other combination of visual elements. You could explore other aspects of your work, for example, looking at the social and cultural contexts of your chosen topic or theme.

In your explorations, you should aim to use a wide range of different media and materials. This range should include both two-dimensional (eg painting and drawing) and three-dimensional (eg clay, textiles and plaster) media.

Documentation

You should show in your work how you arrived at your result – document the process. In a GCSE Art and Design examination, you will be awarded marks for evidence of your artistic development, and of the process you went through, even if the end result is disappointing. You should show evidence of how you changed your work in light of your exploration of the materials and of the topic you are working on.

Presentation

You should clearly communicate your ideas and your intentions – your work, including all of your planning and preparation work, should be self-explanatory. Make sure that all of your work is presented to a high standard and clearly labelled. A high standard includes being clean and free of fingerprints, creases and glue.

Your portfolio

Your portfolio is your folder of work. It should contain a selection of the range of things that you have done in Art and Design, including your preparatory work. Look after it and ensure that it fulfils its function of protecting your work. Your work should be handled carefully and, wherever possible, mounted. It is a good idea to keep a photographic record of any three-dimensional work.

When you have to present coursework for assessment, be selective and ensure that you show your best work, but bear in mind that what you think is your best is not necessarily the same as what others might think – so take advice!

Get into the habit of keeping your preliminary work – mount and label it. This is especially useful if it helps show the process you went through to achieve a particular final piece.

The controlled test

The controlled test is the non-coursework part of the examination, done within a specified time limit. The controlled test part of the GCSE Art and Design examination varies slightly depending upon the examination board. Some boards will give just one theme, such as 'growth' or 'movement'; others will give a choice of questions or starting points.

You will receive the paper well in advance of the examination (usually four weeks) and you must use this time to prepare carefully with appropriate preliminary studies. All of the work done during this preliminary period must be handed in alongside your test piece. It is often a good idea to mount work (although not elaborately) and include written notes.

This work will be assessed according to the assessment objectives: investigation, experimentation, documentation and presentation.

When you know which question or theme to do, you will find it useful to brainstorm ideas. For example, if the theme or key term in your examination paper is 'distortion', you could begin by thinking about the theme and writing down everything that comes into your head:

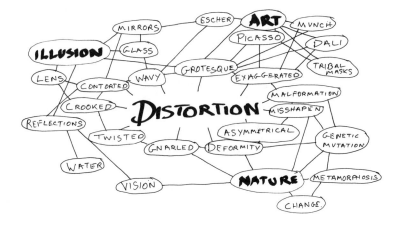

Several brainstorming sessions might be necessary before you come up with something you can develop. It is important that you don't just work with the first idea that comes into your head.

What examiners will look for

Use this checklist when you are preparing for your examination. Your work as a whole should show evidence of:

- your ability to explore and analyse what you see, and to interpret the world around you in a creative way; this might include drawings from observation, as well as imaginative and expressive work in different media which conveys ideas and feelings

- work that is skilfully produced, showing control of the media and a sensitive use of the visual elements

- experimentation with various media

- research, using a wide range of sources, and the ability to select and use the material in a coherent way

- planning and making informed judgements about how to develop and refine your work

- your awareness of different kinds of artwork from different times and places

- knowledge of different ways that artists have produced artwork

- well-thought-through opinions about art which can be justified, using a wide-ranging and specialist art vocabulary, in an appropriate way.

You can see from the above that you will only gain a good grade if you pay attention to the *process* of art-making as well as the *product*.

Glossary

Note: Where a term in the glossary is referred to in another entry, it is shown there in bold.

ABORIGINAL ART

Aboriginal means the original inhabitants of a place. Many people use the term for the Aboriginal people of Australia, whose culture is probably the oldest continuous culture in the history of mankind. Australian Aboriginal art is characterised by its use of earth colours and by the recurrence of particular symbols, often representing journeys. Dots of **paint** are used extensively and give Australian Aboriginal art its characteristic look.

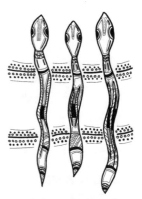

An image in the style of Aboriginal art

ABSTRACT ART

This usually refers to work which is not representational. The artist's work is often concerned with the depiction of ideas which have no basis in everyday reality.

ACRYLIC

Acrylic **paint** can be used thickly, like **oil paint**, or watered down to be like **watercolour**. It dries very quickly and, once dry, it is waterproof. Brushes must be washed out immediately with water after use.

AERIAL PERSPECTIVE

Sometimes called atmospheric perspective, this is a method which artists use to convey a feeling of distance in a painting by varying the colour: the **tone** becomes paler, the **hue** becomes bluer and the **saturation** is less intense.

AESTHETICS

Aesthetics is a branch of philosophy which is mainly concerned with making judgements about what art is and is not. It is sometimes considered to be concerned with understanding the nature of beauty.

ANALOGOUS

In a **colour wheel**, colours which are next to each other, such as red and orange, are analogous. It is the opposite of **complementary**.

ARMATURE

An armature is the framework around which a clay, plaster, paper or soft **sculpture** is modelled.

ARTEFACT

This word comes from the Latin words *ars* meaning art and *fact* meaning made. It is something made with skill by someone.

BATIK

Batik is a method of printing on textiles which is based on using wax to resist dye.

BISQUE-FIRED

Sometimes referred to as biscuit-fired, this refers to clay which has been heated in a **kiln** to a high temperature (around 900°c). At this temperature, the clay undergoes a chemical change and fuses – it cannot be dissolved in water, unlike unfired clay. This means that once an item is fired, it can remain in that state for thousands of years if left undisturbed. Once a piece of clayware has been bisque-fired, it can be coated with a liquid **glaze** and given a **glaze** firing.

CANVAS

Canvas is a heavy woven fabric, made of linen or heavy cotton. It is the preferred painting surface for many artists using **oil** or **acrylic paint**. It needs to be prepared by tacking it onto a frame (known as a **stretcher**) and **primed**.

CERAMICS

Ceramics covers products and **processes** involving clay (and glass) which involve the use of a **kiln**.

CHARCOAL

Charcoal is a piece of burnt twig, usually willow, used for drawing. It needs to be **fixed** to stop it smudging. Interesting effects can be achieved by using charcoal in conjunction with white chalk, to give a range of tonal values.

CHIAROSCURO

This is the dramatic effect of light and dark in a painting to create atmosphere and depth. See the work of Caravaggio (1573-1610) and Rembrandt (1606-1669).

CLIP ART

Clip art is professionally-prepared graphics which are available for use with various computer programs.

COLLAGE

The term collage is derived from the French *coller* meaning to glue or stick. It is a two-dimensional technique (when three-dimensional, it is called *assemblage*), usually involving gluing down bits of paper, fabric or other material to create or add to an artwork.

A Man in Armour by **Rembrandt** displays chiaroscuro

COLLAGRAPH

A collagraph is a print, usually using an **intaglio process** (that is, the print comes from beneath the surface, as in **etching**). It is based on gluing down paper and card of different textures (hence *collagraph*, as in **collage**) and then inking it up and taking a print from it.

COLOUR WHEEL

A colour wheel is a circular chart which is divided into segments, each showing the main **primary** and **secondary colours**. The colours which are least alike in terms of **hue (complementary)**, such as blue and orange, are on opposite sides of the wheel. Colours which are similar (**analogous**), such as blue and violet, are next to each other. See page 74 for an example of a colour wheel.

COMPLEMENTARY

Not to be confused with complimentary! Complementary colours are those which are least alike. They appear opposite each other in a **colour wheel**.

COMPOSITION

A composition is something which is put together – an arrangement of different elements. In art, the **visual elements** are combined by paying attention to things such as balance, harmony, rhythm and contrast to give a unified whole. Sometimes, composition is used to refer to one piece of artwork, such as a painting.

CONTEMPORARY ART

Contemporary art is artwork which is currently being produced by living artists. It is often concerned with contemporary issues and can take many forms.

CONTENT

The content of an artwork is its subject matter. In a painting, for example, the content is what is depicted, such as buildings, people and plants, or what it appears to be about. A work of art is often said to be made up from two elements: **form** and content.

DIGITAL CAMERA

Pictures taken by digital cameras are stored in computer memory rather than on film. A sensor in the camera converts light into digital data which can be stored on a floppy disk or card and loaded into a computer.

EASEL

An easel is a structure, usually wooden, for holding a painting while it is in progress. It normally has three legs and a ledge for holding brushes and other tools.

ETCHING

Etching usually refers to a printmaking **process** whereby a design drawn on metal is 'etched' or eaten away by acid.

EYE LEVEL

In **linear perspective**, the eye level is an imaginary line which corresponds to a viewer's height relative to the horizon line. All **vanishing points** would converge on the eye level.

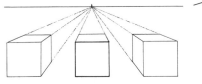

FIX

Charcoal and chalk **pastel** work needs to be 'fixed' to stop it smudging. This can be done by spraying with a fixative or hairspray.

FORM

The form of an artwork is the overall unity of its **visual elements**. Form is sometimes used to refer to the **three-dimensional** aspect of an artwork, as opposed to shape, which is seen as referring to the **two-dimensional** aspect.

FROTTAGE

Frottage is where an artwork is made by taking rubbings from a surface.

GLAZE

The word *glaze* is related to the word *glass*. It is a term used in **ceramics** which refers to the thin, shiny coating which is fused onto fired clay (see **bisque-fired**).

GOUACHE

Gouache is a type of water-based **paint** which is quite thick and opaque. It can be used to give colours which are flat yet saturated.

GRAFFITI

This is the plural of *graffito*, from the Italian for 'scratch'. It has come to mean writing, spraying, drawing or scratching words or images onto a (usually public) surface, such as a wall. Some graffiti is witty and humorous and done with some degree of skill; unfortunately, most, especially the 'tag' form, which is basically a stylised signature, is simply childish and destructive.

GRAPHIC DESIGN

Graphic design is concerned with the communication of ideas and information by visual means. It is usually commercial in nature, taking the form of, for example, advertisements and product labels.

GROUND

Ground has three different meanings in art: it can refer to the foundation base for a painting (for example, **acrylic paint** on **canvas**); in **etching**, it refers to the acid-resistant waxy layer on metal which is scratched through to reveal the metal to be etched away with acid; it also refers to the background area of a picture, as opposed to the main objects or figures.

HUE

Hue is an aspect of colour which is concerned with the yellowness, redness or blueness of a particular colour. There are over 150 discernible hues.

INTAGLIO

Intaglio is a type of print where the image comes from beneath the surface of the printing block (sometimes made of plastic, as in drypoint).

KILN

A kiln is a kind of oven used to bake clay. It 'fires' at very high temperatures and causes clay to chemically change, so that, once fired, it cannot be made soft again.

LANDSCAPE

In painting and other **two-dimensional** works, landscapes are scenic pictures, either taken from nature or invented. It is also sometimes used to refer to the proportions of a painting or piece of paper – landscape is width longer than height, whereas **portrait** is height longer than width.

LINE

Line is one of the **visual elements**. It is the path of a moving point, such as a pen, pencil or brush. In your work, it is important to vary the quality of lines, making them bold and heavy or light and delicate to suggest different things. Line can be used to give the impression of different **textures** and **tones**, as well as simply showing where the edge of an object meets space – remember that objects do not have outlines in real life.

LINEAR PERSPECTIVE

Linear perspective is a drawing system which is based on lines converging on one or more **vanishing points** on the viewer's eye level.

MAQUETTE

A maquette is a small-scale model, made as a **three-dimensional** preliminary 'sketch'.

MASTERPIECE

Originally, a masterpiece was a test piece given to an apprentice to see if they were worthy of being a master in their craft. It is now usually applied to an artwork which is considered to be outstanding and the best of its kind.

MEDIA

Media is the plural of *medium*. In this context, it refers to the substance or **process** you use to produce an artwork. For example, an oil painting is painted using the medium of **oil paint**. **Paint**, ink and clay are different media. It is also used to refer to something which binds **pigments** together, such as oil, **acrylic**, gum, egg-white or wax.

MONOPRINT

Sometimes called a monotype print, a monoprint is a **process** whereby one print at a time is taken. Using a piece of paper lying face down on an inked-up surface, an image is drawn on the back; the pressure of the drawing picks up ink on the front with a resulting image.

A monoprint

MONTAGE

This term is from the French *monter* meaning to fix objects into or onto something. A montage is a **two-dimensional** artwork made up from overlapping images; in **photomontage**, only photographs are used.

MOTIF

Motif usually refers to a repeated **visual element** or combination of elements found in a **pattern** or **composition**. It can also refer to the dominant theme or idea in an artwork.

OIL PAINT

Oil paint is made from **pigments** mixed with oils. Brushes and palettes need to be cleaned with white spirit or turpentine, which can, along with linseed oil, be used to thin it. It can be applied very thickly with a knife as well as a brush (this technique is called *impasto*) and is very slow-drying (in the case of impasto works, it can take many weeks).

PAINT

Paint is made up from three main things: **pigment**, to give it colour; a **medium** (such as oil), which is used to support the **pigment**; and something to thin it down, such as water or turpentine.

PALETTE

A palette is a portable tray which artists use for mixing colours. The term 'artist's palette' refers also to the range of colours which an artist uses. A *palette knife* is a flexible, blunt knife used for both mixing and applying **paint**.

PAPIER MÂCHÉ

Papier mâché is a material made from torn-up paper (often newspaper) soaked in water with the addition of glue or paste.

PASTEL

Pastel crayons are made from **pigment** and gum. Chalk pastels easily smudge and need to be **fixed**. Oil pastels have an oil to bind them and are easier to blend; they do not smudge as easily but, like **oil paint**, they take a long time to dry. The term *pastel* also refers to colours which are delicate **tints**.

Pattern

PASTICHE

Pastiche literally means things pasted together. In an art context, it refers to an imitation of someone else's style.

PATTERN

Pattern has three main meanings: a decorative design, usually of a repeated **motif** or figure; the **composition** or layout of an artwork; and the model or mould used for casting. In the first sense, visual forms, or **motifs**, are repeated, often in a systematic manner, such as in the repeated geometric forms found in Islamic art.

PHOTOMONTAGE

Photomontage is a pictorial **composition** made up from an arrangement of photographs or parts of photographs, often combined to give a different overall effect (for example, putting photographs of animals' heads onto photographs of human bodies). See the work of John Heartfield (1891-1968) who used photomontages effectively as anti-Nazi propaganda in the 1930s.

PIGMENT

Pigment is the substance in **paint** and ink which gives it colour.

PORTRAIT

A portrait is an artwork which represents a particular person (or sometimes animal), often showing just the head and shoulders. A picture or piece of paper which is 'portrait way up' has a height longer than its width.

PRIMARY COLOUR

Red, blue and yellow are the primary colours in art; they cannot be mixed from other colours. When two of them are mixed together, a **secondary colour** is formed. In physics, or where coloured light is used, the primary colours are blue, red and green. In printing, the primary colours are magenta (a kind of pink), cyan (a kind of blue) and yellow.

PRIME

To prime a **canvas** or other surface is to make it suitable for painting upon by providing a white base which gives the right amount of absorbency. Priming is done with primer, a white coating known as **ground**. **Canvases** can be bought ready-primed.

PROCESS

The procedures that one goes through in creating an artwork are known as the process, for example, the process of printmaking.

PUG/PUGMILL

To pug, which is usually done in a machine called a pugmill, is to squash clay in readiness for use. See also **wedge**.

RELIEF

In printmaking, a relief print is one that is taken from the surface of an image, either gouged out as in a linoprint, or built up, as in a string print (where string is glued onto a piece of card). Relief also refers to a **sculptural composition,** where an image is carved out to stand above the background.

SATURATION

Saturation is an aspect of colour concerned with its purity, richness or brilliance. Saturation can be high intensity or low intensity. It is sometimes referred to in terms of its brightness or dullness.

SCALE

Scale refers to the relative proportion of one thing to another. Something which is drawn on a scale of a tenth is ten times smaller than the original.

SCANNER

Images (or text) can be placed on a scanner and converted into digital information which can be fed into a computer.

SCREEN PRINT

Sometimes called silk screen printing, this is a **process** of printmaking based on using stencils. The ink is forced through a fine mesh (the 'silk') with a **squeegee** onto the receiving paper underneath the screen.

SCULPTURE

A sculpture is a **three-dimensional** artwork (produced by a sculptor). Sculptures can be carved or modelled, using a wide range of materials. In **contemporary art,** light is sometimes used; boundaries are also blurred between traditional approaches to sculpture and performance.

SECONDARY COLOUR

In colour theory, secondary colours for **pigments** are orange, green and violet (or purple); they can be mixed from two **primary colours.** Using **paint,** red and yellow will make orange; blue and yellow will make green; and violet can be made from blue and red.

SFUMATO

This is from an Italian word, and is used in painting to describe the gradual, soft changes in **tone**, from dark to light. It is a useful term to describe mellow, atmospheric effects, for example, in the paintings of Leonardo da Vinci.

SGRAFFITO

Sometimes known as **graffito**, this term refers mainly to the technique of scratching away a surface to reveal other layers of material underneath. Originally, this was a popular art form in 16th-century Italy (the word means 'scratched drawing' in Italian) which involved cutting away plaster to reveal a different colour underneath. Nowadays, the term is often used to refer to work done in **ceramics**, where **slip** is cut through to reveal a different surface.

SHADE

A shade is an aspect of colour which has had black added (and is therefore a darker **tone**). In this respect, it can be said to be the 'opposite' of **tint**.

SLIP

The word *slip* is derived from the Old English word *slipa* which meant 'slime'. It is very fine clay mixed with water. It can be used for decorative effects or, more commonly, as a kind of glue to fix two pieces of clay together (the surfaces should be scratched or scored first).

SQUEEGEE

A squeegee is a thick piece of rubber set into a piece of wood. It is used for squeezing printing ink through the screen used in **screen printing**.

STENCIL

A stencil is a thin sheet of metal, cardboard or plastic in which a design (or letters and numbers) is cut. The uncut areas act as a mask. Stencils can be used in **screen printing**, where the masked part prevents the printing ink from going through the screen.

STILL LIFE

Still life is a painting or drawing of a group of objects, which have been selected by the artist.

STRETCHER

A stretcher is a wooden framework upon which an artist's **canvas** is stretched and tacked.

SYMMETRY

Symmetry is related to the idea of balance, and refers to parts of a figure being the same as other parts. A typical example of symmetry would be a 'perfectly proportioned face', or a building which is exactly the same on either side of a central dividing line.

TEMPERA

Tempera is a kind of **paint** which is water-soluble. It is traditionally made from egg.

TENEBRISM

Tenebrism is derived from an Italian word meaning dark or gloomy. It is used to refer to the technique of painting using dark and dramatic **tones**. Paintings which show tenebrism tend to have more shadows than those showing **chiaroscuro**.

TEXTURE

Texture is the surface quality of an object. In art, it can refer to an illusion of texture, for example, in a painting which shows the smoothness of a child's face and the rough surface of a tree. It can also refer to actual texture, as in a **collage**. In your own work, you can achieve different textures by adding different materials to your **paint,** or by incorporating things such as fragments of hard clay, sawdust or sand into the **medium** you are using.

THREE-DIMENSIONAL

Sometimes written or said as '3-D', this refers to artworks which are solid – having height, width and depth – such as models and **sculptures**.

TINT

A tint is an aspect of colour which has had white added (and is therefore a lighter **tone**). In this respect, it can be said to be the 'opposite' of **shade**.

TONE

Tone is normally seen as one aspect of colour, concerned with its lightness or darkness.

TWO-DIMENSIONAL

Sometimes written or said as '2-D', this refers to artworks which have a height and width but no obvious thickness or depth, such as paintings, drawings and prints.

VANISHING POINTS

In **linear perspective**, a vanishing point is the point where imaginary lines which recede from objects converge on the eye level.

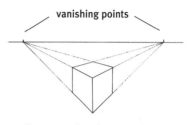

vanishing points

VIEWFINDER

A viewfinder is a piece of card with a small rectangular shape cut in the centre, used to isolate parts of a scene or picture.

VISUAL (AND TACTILE) ELEMENTS

This is a phrase which is sometimes used to cover all of the parts we can see (visual) or touch (tactile) in a work of art, such as: colour, **form, line, pattern, texture** and **tone**.

WATERCOLOUR

Watercolour is a kind of **paint** which is mixed with water, either from a tube or a hard slab. It is usually applied onto heavy paper in translucent washes (that is, you can see the paper through it). As it is often applied onto a damp surface, it is better for the paper to be previously **stretched** so as not to cause buckling. When it is dry, it cannot be easily altered.

WEDGE

To wedge clay is to manipulate and pound it until all of the air bubbles come out. This ensures that a finished piece will not explode in the **kiln** due to air expanding inside it.

ZIP DRIVE

A zip drive is a removable device which can be attached to your computer. Its function is the same as a floppy disk drive, but it holds much larger amounts of information – useful when saving images.

Further resources

Useful books

Barley, N (1994) *Smashing Pots – feats of clay from Africa*, London: British Museum Press

DES (1986) *Safety in Practical Studios*, London: HMSO

Gage, J (1993) *Colour and Culture – Practice and Meaning from Antiquity to Abstraction*, London: Thames and Hudson

Goldfinger, E (1991) *Human Anatomy for Artists – the elements of form*, Oxford: Oxford University Press

Jewell, R (1995) *African Designs* (British Museum Pattern Book), London: British Museum Press

Papanek, V (1995) *Design for the Real World: Human Ecology and Social Change*, Chicago: Academy Publishers

Papanek, V (1995) *The Green Imperative: Natural Design for the Real World*, London: Thames and Hudson

Phaidon (1994) *The Art Book*, London: Phaidon Press

Smith, S and Ten Nolt, H F (Eds) (1985) *The Artist's Manual*, London: Macdonald

West, K (1995) *Creative Perspective for Artists and Designers*, London: The Herbert Press

Wilcox, M (1987) *Blue and Yellow Don't Make Green*, Perth: Colour School of Publishing

Places to see art

Arnolfini Gallery, 16 Narrow Quay, Bristol, BS1 4QA, Tel 0117 9299191

Aspex Gallery, 27 Brougham Road, Portsmouth, PO5 4PA, Tel 0239 2812121

The Grizedale Society, Grizedale, Hawkshead, Ambleside, Cumbria, LA22 0TJ, Tel 01229 860291

Hayward Gallery, South Bank Centre, London, SE1 8XZ,
Tel 020 7960 4242

ICA (Institute Of Contemporary Art), 12 Carlton House Terrace,
London, SW1Y 5AH, Tel 020 7930 0493

Ikon Gallery, 1 Oozells Square, Brindley Place, Birmingham,
Tel 0121 2480708

John Hansard Gallery, University of Southampton, Highfield, S017 1BJ,
Tel 0238 0592158

Kettles Yard, Castle Street, Cambridge, CB3 0AQ, Tel 01223 352124

Leeds City Art Gallery, Leeds City Centre, LS1 3AA, Tel 0113 2478254

Liverpool Tate, Albert Dock, Liverpool, L3 4BB, Tel 0151 7027400

The Lowry, Salford, Tel 0161 8762042

Manchester City Art Galleries, Room 1025, Town Hall Extension,
Lloyd Street, Manchester, M60 2LA Tel 0161 2341456

Museum of Modern Art Oxford, 30 Pembroke Street, Oxford, OX1 1BP,
Tel 0186 5722733

National Gallery, Trafalgar Square, London, WC2N 5DN,
Tel 020 7747 2885

St Ives Tate, Porthmeor Beach, St Ives, Cornwall, TR26 1TG,
Tel 01736 796226

Tate Britain, Millbank, London, SW1P 4RG, Tel 020 7887 8008

Tate Modern, Bankside, London, SE1 9TG, Tel 020 7887 8008

The Yorkshire Sculpture Park, Bretton Hall, Wakefield, West Yorkshire,
WF4 4LG, Tel 01924 830679

Web sites

In addition to the 24-hour museum at www.24hourmuseum.org.uk, the following might be of interest:

ArtNet — http://www.artnet.com/

Arts Electronica — http://www.electronica.com/

The Cooper Hewitt National Design Museum (Smithsonian) —
http://www.ndm.si.edu/

The Design Council — http://www.design-council.org.uk/

Dia Centre for the Arts — http://www.diacenter.org/

Digital Jungle (graffiti art in London) — http://www.graffiti.org/dj/

The Institute of Contemporary Arts (ICA) — http://www.ica.org.uk/

Institute of International Visual Arts — http://www.iniva.org/

Lisson Gallery — http://www.lisson.co.uk/

The Louvre Gallery, France — http://www.louvre.fr/

Museum of Modern Art, New York (MoMA) — http://www.moma.org/

Rhizome art magazine — http://www.rhizome.com/

Suppliers of materials

Alec Tiranti LTD, Sculptors' Catalogue, tools, materials and studio equipment, Tel 0118 9302775

Bath Potters Supplies, ceramic and clayware, Tel 01225 337046

Berol (Sanford UK), pens and markers, Tel 01553 761221

Budget Paper Supplies, Tel 01733 252868

Daler Rowney, paint and canvas, Tel 01344 424621

Dryad, specialists in craft materials, Tel 0116 2510405

Espo Ltd, everything from pencils to printing paper, Tel 0116 2657878

Inmac, PC hardware and software products, Tel 0870 5168672

NES Arnold, general supplies of paper, inks, pens, markers and textiles equipment, Tel 0870 6000193

Potclays Ltd, ceramics and clayware, Tel 01782 219816

Seawhite, high quality sketchbooks, Tel 01403 711633

Technomatic, PC hardware, software and supplies, Tel 0845 602896